SILENCE, SOBRIETY, SOLIDARITY

SILENCE, SOBRIETY, SOLIDARITY

Living with a
Contemplative Heart

Michael Downey

FOREWORD BY
Bernardus Peeters, OCSO
Trappist Abbot General

Paulist Press
New York / Mahwah, NJ

Cover image by andre2013/depositphotos.com
Cover and book design by Lynn Else

Library of Congress Cataloging-in-Publication Data
Names: Downey, Michael, author.
Title: Silence, sobriety, solidarity: living with a contemplative heart / Michael Downey ; foreword by Bernardus Peeters, OCSO, Abbot General of the Order of Cistercians of the Strict Observance, Trappists.
Description: New York ; Mahwah, NJ : Paulist Press, [2024] | Includes bibliographical references. | Summary: "An accessible understanding of prayer inviting the reader into the deepest kind of prayer in silence, sobriety, and solidarity"—Provided by publisher.
Identifiers: LCCN 2023036648 (print) | LCCN 2023036649 (ebook) | ISBN 9780809156900 (paperback) | ISBN 9780809188420 (ebook)
Subjects: LCSH: Spirituality—Catholic Church. | Silence—Religious aspects—Catholic Church. | Prayer—Catholic Church.
Classification: LCC BX2350.65 .D675 2024 (print) | LCC BX2350.65 (ebook)| DDC 248.088/282—dc23/eng/20240126
LC record available at https://lccn.loc.gov/2023036648
LC ebook record available at https://lccn.loc.gov/2023036649

ISBN 978-0-8091-5690-0 (paperback)
ISBN 978-0-8091-8842-0 (ebook)

Published by Paulist Press
997 Macarthur Boulevard
Mahwah, New Jersey 07430
www.paulistpress.com

Printed and bound in the
United States of America

To my first teachers
The Sisters, Servants of the Immaculate Heart of Mary
Immaculata, Pennsylvania
who instilled in me the love of learning
and the desire for God

CONTENTS

FOREWORD

*A*fter a long and arduous meeting in the Vatican, I leave the building that houses the Dicastery (compare it to a ministry) for Religious Life. As Abbot General of a worldwide religious order in the Roman Catholic Church, I sometimes have to be here to discuss mostly difficult and painful topics that deal with crises in the lives of a community or individuals.

I emerge from the building and find myself at the edge of the immense Saint Peter's Square with its embracing colonnade by the baroque artist Bernini. I have not yet had time to breathe in the fresh Roman spring air. A young woman with a strong American accent and with a thumbed King James Bible under her arm addresses me and asks if I am a Roman Catholic priest. She may have assumed that I am a priest because I was wearing my Trappist habit. She wants to talk to a priest about the fact that Protestants believe that faith alone justifies and that we Catholics think we are also justified by our good works.

"My God, does this have to happen now?" I want to go home, away from the bustle of the city. But then

I suddenly remember the words from the Gospel: "Then Jesus stopped" (Luke 18:40). I decide to stop and listen to the fierce argument of the woman. At first she hesitates with her words, going slowly because someone is willing to listen to her. Trying to follow her argument, all sorts of answers fly through my mind, and I find myself not even listening anymore. Back to Silence—back to attention. "Staying still in the silence I encounter the One whose name above all naming is Love."

Eventually I get the chance to say something. By now I had thought of explaining to her that this is a false opposition between grace and good works. I wanted to tell her about that groundbreaking 1999 ecumenical document—to which, unfortunately, almost no one in the Christian world pays attention—in which Lutherans and Catholics joined each other in a common statement about faith and works. But all I say is: "If God has justified me by faith then he has also given me certain signposts that I may use to preserve and keep alive this faith, this grace." She looked at me kindly and silently, then turned and disappeared into the crowd.

This story would fit perfectly into Michael Downey's book on Silence, Sobriety, and Solidarity. Drawing from the Cistercian/Trappist tradition, the author starts from experience. In experience, he constantly searches for a glimpse of God. One notices in this attitude to life his many years of friendship and commitment to Cistercian/Trappist life. This is proof that the Cistercian charism does not belong only to monks and nuns in their monasteries but is a gift that is also given to others who live it in different ways and walks of life.

From the beginning, the Cistercians have sought to define their charism with the words: "So that God may be glorified in all things." Michael Downey gives the reader tools to bring glory to God through daily experience. That is a life of unceasing prayer where it is not about the quantity of prayers but the quality of being attentive to God in everything and everyone. This book is a quiet, sober, and solid signpost to guide us on the way to an attentive life in God's presence.

In everyone's life, even in the life of monks and nuns, or in that of a religious order, a situation can arise in which we experience a crisis. This is a time when everything seems to be turned upside down. What was familiar is suddenly no longer taken for granted. In a crisis, you often don't know the way out. In that darkness, a prayer often naturally rises to the surface: "God, come to my aid!" (see Ps 70:1). This is the prayer par excellence of the monastic who tries to pray without ceasing. It is a prayer out of the silence of not knowing. It is a prayer that is sober because in the darkness of every crisis, every word seems almost too much. It is a prayer in solidarity with all people, with all creation, so often caught up and on the brink of being crushed by crisis.

This kind of prayer in Silence, Sobriety, and Solidarity brings us more deeply into the mystery of Christ's Pasch, participating *even now* in his life, suffering, dying, and death, but also his resurrection!

This slim volume helps us to follow the signposts of Silence, Sobriety, and Solidarity in order to let everlasting prayer flow into our hearts in all the events, encounters, and circumstances of our lives. Here we have not one more "magnificent distraction" but a wonderful help to learn to listen to the heartbeat of God.

Dum spiro, spero—While I breathe, I hope.

Dom Bernardus Peeters, OCSO
Abbot General
Order of Cistercians of the Strict Observance

PREFACE

*S*hortly after his election as Abbot General of the Order of Cistercians of the Strict Observance (OCSO, also known as Trappists and Trappistines) on February 11, 2022, Bernardus Peeters, formerly Abbot of Our Lady of Koningshoeven Abbey, Tilburg, the Netherlands, sent an open letter to the men and women of the Order. Having spent longish periods of time at a monastery not far from Tilburg, I was fortunate to receive a copy of the letter as it was circulated.

In that letter, the Abbot General draws attention to three themes: Silence, Sobriety, Solidarity. These three were part of the vision for the renewal of monastic life at Tilburg, and the newly elected Abbot General sets them forward as part of the vision for the rejuvenation of the Trappists/Trappistines. In this circular letter and in other more recent letters, reports, and conferences, he hearkens back to these three. Like no Abbot General before him, Bernardus Peeters states plainly two realities: (1) the OCSO is not only "precarious" and "vulnerable" (well-worn words of previous Abbots General) at this moment in its history, but it is in crisis; (2) the objective of the various monasteries in the Order should not be to keep individual monasteries open but, rather, to find ways to assure the flourishing of the Cistercian/Trappist charism in the various regions and countries where the monks and nuns live.

In reading the Abbot General's words, I sensed once again a summons to a reconfiguration of the Cistercian charism "outside the walls." This volume is, in part, intended as a contribution to such a reconfiguration. Without question, the Cistercian charism is a gift to the Order of Cistercians of the Strict Observance. But it is not theirs alone. Rooted in the primacy of the incarnation, this charism is a gift by which we move with the Spirit of God who moves within us to pray without ceasing (1 Thess 5:17) or, better, to live prayerfully.

While in Rome for the canonization of Charles de Foucauld in mid-May 2022, I met for several hours with Bernardus Peeters to discuss these three dimensions: Silence, Sobriety, Solidarity. At the conclusion of our meeting, I asked if he thought it appropriate for me to craft an essay on these three themes. He encouraged me to do so.

In the intervening months, I have found that a small volume would be more fitting for what is to be said. And so, this small volume offers a treatment of Silence, Sobriety, Solidarity within the context of an understanding of prayer as well as the hurdles we face in our own time and place as we respond to the gift and task not only to pray but to pray without ceasing: living prayerfully moment by moment.

Each chapter begins with a reflection, or a rumination, intended to evoke a sense of how we might live in Silence, Sobriety, and Solidarity in everything. The volume concludes with a final rumination intended to capture something of the spirit of this slim volume.

ACKNOWLEDGMENTS

A contemplative heart is a grateful heart. And this heart has so much for which to be grateful, beyond the telling of it. But let me try.

The first word of thanks goes to Bernardus Peeters, Abbot General of the Order of Cistercians of the Strict Observance (Trappists/Trappistines). His vision, his dream, for the future of monastic and contemplative life prompted me to take my poised pen and put it to paper. Without his encouragement, my pen would still be poised in midair.

Raniero Hoffman of New Camaldoli Hermitage was an energetic and insightful conversation partner in the early stages of writing.

Patrick Markey of the Focolare Movement has once again reviewed my work as it neared completion and offered helpful suggestions for improvement.

Eileen E. O'Brien, a former student and also friend over the years and across the miles, has, once again, cast her eagle eye on my work with meticulous precision and keen theological sense.

Some of the writing took place in Saigon, where the words of Graham Greene first echoed in my heart nearly twenty years ago: "They say you come to Vietnam and you understand love in a few minutes....And nothing is ever the same again."

As on several occasions in the past, the bulk of the writing took place at the Trappist Abbey of Mont-des-Cats in Franco-Flanders. More than forty years ago I was first welcomed by the monks of Mont-des-Cats, and again and again they have given me time and space to be *chez moi* for retreat, solitude, and writing.

As this slim volume was being finalized, I was asked in all sincerity: "What is the role of an editor in publishing?" My reply: "My editor is everything!" That is most assuredly true of Donna M. Crilly, senior academic editor at Paulist Press.

CHAPTER ONE

LIVING PRAYERFULLY

The celebrations of the Lunar New Year 2023 have come to a close in Vietnam. The quiet of the streets of Ho Chi Minh City, also known as Saigon, signaled that something was not quite right. Quiet. Once called the Pearl of the Orient during the French occupation of Indochina (Cambodia, Laos, and Vietnam), except for the three days of the Lunar New Year, Saigon is relentlessly exhilarating. Intoxicating, in both senses of the term.

Most everyone in Vietnam—the second largest exporter of coffee worldwide—rises early here. Long before the light breaks I have found a little coffee stand and the old woman offers me a plastic kiddy chair with my strong blacker-than-coal coffee. The French are gone, but the blackness of the coffee is one of the traces they left behind. I watch as the streets begin to fill with motorbikes, sellers, shoppers, begging children, pleading children. Every white face in Vietnam is thought to mask a millionaire.

As the streets begin to pulse with honking motorbikes and breath-stopping moment-by-moment traffic near-misses, Graham Greene's words in The Quiet American *echo:*

"They say, whatever you are looking for you will find here."

"They say you come to Vietnam and you understand love in a few minutes." "The rest has got to be lived."

"Something happens, as you knew it would. And nothing is ever the same again."

"Everything is so intense: the food, the colors, the rain."

And the smells. The flesh. Everywhere there is pulsing bodiliness. Sheer aliveness. The thing about life is that there is so much of it!

The curmudgeonly Irish cynic in me questions. True, God became flesh. But does God really love eeeeeveeeeeryyyyybody?

As on each morning, I try to be alert to the presence of God. Most times, I only get a faint glimpse of some traces here and there. In the darkness of morning's night, I remember the ways in which many who have gone before us have encountered the presence of the living God. It is my gift and task here and now in a pale blue kiddy chair, drinking stronger-than-stone black coffee, to be alert to God's constant coming in this now sullied and sordid Pearl of the Orient.

Francis of Assisi encountered God in the putrid body of an isolated leper cast to the outskirts of Assisi, impelling him to see everyone as a brother or sister in Christ, especially the last, the lost, the littlest, and the least. His eye turned to Brother Sun, all creation, and every living creature, even the Wolf of Gubbio, as his brothers and sisters.

Even Death he called his Sister. In all—everyone and every living thing—Francis recognized the possibility of encountering the presence of the living God.

In a similar vein, Agnes Bojaxhiu, later known as Mother Teresa of Calcutta, recognized a "call within a call." She asked to leave her religious congregation, the Dublin-based Sisters of Loreto, prompted by her visual encounter with the desperately poor and dying in the streets of Calcutta where she was stationed in the Loreto Convent Boarding School for daughters of the wealthy. This encounter prompted her deeper desire for real, flesh and blood, bodily encounter with "the poorest of the poor" in the filth and bodily decay clogging the streets of Calcutta.

The wandering French aristocrat Charles de Foucauld, spendthrift, womanizer, explorer, soldier, first encountered God in the prayerfulness of the Muslims he encountered while on military assignment in the French-colonized Sahara. On return to France, he made a confession to a parish priest and received the Eucharist. Brother Charles is now a canonized saint whose Catholic faith was stirred in his encounter with God in Muslims at prayer in the wide openness of the Sahara.

The Christ he encountered was the One who lived in hiddenness and obscurity at Nazareth, those thirty years at home in Nazareth before he "did" or "taught" or "accomplished" anything. He and his followers continue his legacy by living "Nazareth," the hidden life of Jesus **in** Nazareth, or **at** Nazareth. Brother Charles's followers live Nazareth in small dwellings among the poor in Vietnam, France, the Sahara, the United States, Canada, throughout Africa, and around the world. They seek God in the daily round of very ordinary daily activities, rendering themselves present to the encounter with each and every one of their neighbors, near and far.

In Brother Charles we find someone who learned to encounter God—in the ordinary, in the mundane, in the domestic, in the routine—staying alert to God's constant coming, wherever our own Nazareth may be.

Little attention is given to the fact that Charles (1858–1916) was contemporary to one of the most beloved of Catholic saints, the French Carmelite Thérèse of Lisieux (1873–1897). As children and teens, they breathed the same spiritual air; they drank of the well of the same French Catholic culture.

Consider this: Thérèse encountered God in the palpable love of Jesus and, early on, in Mary. Jesus called her to the "little way," doing small, everyday tasks with great love. This "small agency" draws little attention to oneself. If you scrub the floor, scrub it with love. If you change a diaper, change it with love. If you make love with your spouse, don't be thinking about God, make love with love.

Thérèse is often referred to as the "Little Flower." Some might find her a bit too saccharine. But one deep read of the last months of her life could dispel that notion. Her excruciating dying brought with it a damp enveloping darkness we would now call depression. Yet she maintained enough voice to let those near her know that she was breathing her last in the hope of encountering her love beyond the dark veil: Jesus awaiting his beloved little Thérèse.

Ignatius of Loyola encountered God in Christ as Lord and King to be served by his loyal subject, not in Nazareth or through little acts of love but, rather, by always doing *more (the* magis*) for the greater glory of God, so that in all things God may be glorified.*

The followers of Ignatius seek to find God in all things. In some circles they are said to be contemplatives in action: Pray, then act. But the lesser-known scholar of Jesuit Sources, Joseph F. X. Conwell (1919–2014), while at the Gregorian University prior to and during the Second Vatican Council, focused on the Ignatian notion of "finding God in all things." Conwell maintained that "contemplatives in action" does not reflect the intuition of Ignatius and his first companions.

Later, delving deeply into the work of Jerome Nadal of the first generation of Ignatius's followers, often referred to as "the Ignatian theologian," Conwell makes it plain that the follower of Ignatius is to be "contemplative in prayer, likewise in action." A distinction without a real difference? This distinction makes all the difference. It highlights the contemplative core, not only of prayer, but also of action. In short: Pray contemplatively; act contemplatively.

Ignatius was first and finally a monk at heart. But he would not be bound by monastic disciplines such as communal choral office seven times each day or lifelong stability in one monastery. He recognized that grace is loose in a world where the living God is to be encountered, just as much and as deeply, as in the disciplines of monastic life. The monastic life is a search for the living God. So, too, is the life of the one given to be and become ever more "contemplative in prayer, likewise in action."

The day breaks slowly in Saigon. In the distance from a still quiet corner, I hear the Hymne *by French musician, Clem Beatz. The influence of the French in this, their former colony, can still be discerned, even as it is despised by many, especially those who lived during the colonization of Indochina. Beatz comes from Hyeres, on the southeasternmost coast of France near Corsica and Sardina, and not too far from Malta and the African coast. All those winds blow across the Mediterranean: Italian, African and, via Malta, Arabic. Beatz's music has been described as "between universes." Listen! Begin with* Hymne (https://youtu.be/k2Mb7C8g5bg) *and be lifted into* Bliss (https://youtu.be/F7rxYQSHD-Y).

Hymne *is a wordless wording of guitar strings, chords, keys, and language beyond comprehension. Likewise* Bliss. *The body of the listener cannot help but throb, move as the* Hymne *drops down into that place which is not a place or a space at all. Beatz's* Hymne *evokes the deepest kind of prayer: Wordless wording, language beyond comprehension, pulsing, throbbing in wanting to want the living God. There, even bliss is all too often dark and bitter.*

To another Francis: Jorge Mario Bergoglio, who reminds us that in addition to learning from the great saints, spiritual writers, and the cloud of witnesses who have gone before us, we are to learn also from the saints who may be living next door, working in the next cubicle, sowing seeds and tilling soil in the row next to mine.

Here I remember, indeed encounter, my friend and esteemed, distinguished colleague, theologian Richard René Gaillardetz. As I write, Rick is preparing to make passage. Stricken with pancreatic cancer in February 2022, he continued to write regularly to friends and colleagues. His words are a mystagogy, a revelatory teaching on dying, as he prepared to meet Sister Death. As these pages were going to press, Rick made passage on November 7, 2023. His life is now hidden with Christ in God (Col 3:3).

The silence of the dark morning, the sober breakfast of a single cup of coffee blacker-than-coal, have brought me into the deepest kind of solidarity with a friend who, after a distinguished career of research, writing, and teaching now teaches all of us that even in our dying we might whisper dum spiro, spero: *While I breathe, I hope.*

We are both theological grandsons of sorts, or great-grandsons, or great-great-grandsons of the towering German Jesuit theologian of the twentieth century, Karl Rahner. God is the God beyond our grasp, outside our reach, unknowable and unnamable: Unfathomable Mystery. Rahner's is, put simply, a searching theology. Rick has searched for God his whole life long. His has been a longing, a wanting, a pulsing, throbbing mind and heart with a desire that longs only for its own increase. Simply wanting to want God may be enough. It is the deepmost desire of every human heart: To encounter the living God.

Following an articulation of an understanding of prayer and of the obstacles we face in heeding Paul's admonition to "pray always" (1 Thess 5:17), I reflect on Silence, Sobriety, Solidarity. These are the sine qua non *of living prayerfully, alert to the constant coming of God we long to encounter. Whatever our way and walk in life, the asceticism, the discipline of Silence, Sobriety, Solidarity is absolutely essential to entering into the Unfathomable Mystery of the living God.*

I have a hard time praying, except for all the time. All too often I, like many others, think of prayer as yet one more thing to do in the course of a day, racing from rising to sleeping at breakneck speed, inundated with so much cacophony and clutter. How to find time and space to spend a few minutes with Scripture, meditate on the Gospel of the day, just quietly repeat one of its lines, or whisper a prayer for someone sick or dying.

But then there comes a moment, perhaps a few, in the course of a day when I am all eyes and ears. I am alert to the smile of a cashier working a job at minimum wage, or the sight and sound of my young goddaughter as she delights in learning the sounds of the keys on her mini-piano, or the news of someone dear who, once again, has recognized that he cannot live, let alone thrive, without surrendering—no, abandoning—himself to a Higher Power.

And then there is a glimpse at a flaming red poppy, laden with memory of the thousands who have given their lives so that others might live in freedom. Or that nibble of fragrant French cheese that is a foretaste of the Heavenly Banquet. Or a momentary glimpse of the eyes of someone I love that brings me to the brink of tears. Or a momentary sense of connection with the last, the lost, the littlest, and the least that nearly tears my heart from my chest so that I might be near them—or just one of them—to offer some small comfort. And the stunning awareness that he or she is right in front of me, beside me, behind me. Dare I turn to look at her?

"Pray always" (1 Thess 5:17). No easy matter. It has ever been thus. People in every era are faced with the challenge of praying without ceasing. But prayer without ceasing, living prayerfully, is not primarily a matter of setting time apart, or constantly chattering into God's ear our needs, our wants, our laments and, ever so rarely, our gratitude. It is much more a matter of paying attention, being alert, to God's constant coming in the ordinary events and encounters of our days, in faces of those who cross our path, in the pulse of every living creature, in the azure blue and inky black sky and what lies beyond, in the serene beauty, and often in the unleashed wrath of creation—our Mother Earth—our common home.

Living prayerfully requires first and foremost a hard look at those factors that seem to prevent rather than promote authentic prayer. It takes discipline, a real asceticism, to face the factors in our own time and place that pose serious challenges to those who attempt, not just to "say prayers" alone or with others, privately or communally but, rather, to *live* prayerfully. These hurdles to living prayerfully are not insurmountable, but they must first be identified and recognized for what they are: magnificent distractions. These keep us from entering into the deepest kind of prayer. Once faced squarely there is no ready solution to overcome these obstacles. But a first step is to recognize these challenges as the magnificent distractions they are. Only then can we discern ways to break free of their grip on us, following a daily rigorous, disciplined course of action, so as to move with greater freedom into the deepest kind of prayer whereby we live prayerfully moment by moment.

Prayer of the deepest kind rests in an encounter that stirs up and gives rise to the movement of the human heart toward an ever more complete awareness of God's nearness. Prayer is the lifelong process of learning how to listen long and lovingly to the beating of the heart of God. Christian prayer entails the ongoing participation through the gift of the Spirit/Love in the mystery of the Son/Word who abandoned himself without reserve and with boundless confidence to God, the One he called Father, even and especially in his darkest night: "Into your hands I commend my spirit" (Luke 23:46).

To speak of prayer as a movement of the human heart is not to limit prayer to a region of private, individual feelings or emotions in contrast to other dimensions of the person in relation to another, others, every living creature, and the whole of creation. And *heart* is not to be understood in opposition to the mind, to intellect or reason, even though it may happen that the Spirit/Love of God may move one to act in a way that seems to be counterintuitive to the canons of reason in the strict and formal sense. Consider: It may seem unreasonable for someone to dive into a swelling river to release a complete and utter stranger from a car being engulfed by flooding waters brought on by torrential rains.

Heart describes the deepest, most fundamental center or core of oneself. As such the term is found in the Hebrew (*leb, lebab*), and Christian (*kardia*) Scripture and in the history of Christian spirituality (*cor; cordis affectus*), to describe the whole person, not this or that "part" of the person such as feelings or emotions. *Heart* is the term for "affectivity," which is so much deeper than our affections. Affectivity is so foundational to human life that it is not a stretch to say that the person *is* the heart.

Affectivity describes the very openness of the person, from infancy onward, to be touched by another, others, and God, and to be drawn into relationship with them. Beginning with the infant's openness to his or her mother or primary caregiver, the heart expands and, if properly nurtured, opens to communal and social realities. It is the capacity to be in relationship. And it is also the exercise of this capacity. The heart is that in us that knows, prior to the exercise of intellect or reason, what Pope Francis invites us to see in *Fratelli Tutti*: Everything is related to everything else; everyone is related to everyone else.

When rooted in the heart, even private prayer is not an individual, isolated activity. Prayer may be expressed privately, or individually, in various ways: meditation; private devotion; recitation of the Litany of the Saints or the rosary. For many, prayer finds its fullest expression in the communal prayer of the Christian people, the Eucharistic Liturgy, the communal act of worship in which the Christian community receives and expresses its identity as the Body of Christ.

Recovering the heart as the fundamental openness to be in relation and, as such, the locus of the encounter with another, others, and God, does not imply a privileging of private prayer. Nor does it relegate communal prayer to the periphery. As the relational matrix within each and every one of us, as the capacity and exercise of the capacity to be in relation, the heart is the locus of the encounter with humanity, with other living creatures, with the wider world, and events both past and present. Above all, it is the place or space of encounter with the One whose name above all naming is Love—pouring forth in the naming that can be heard only in that wide open space/place which is not a space/place at all. In Silence: "You are my beloved child. You are my daughter. You are my son. You are mine."

CHAPTER TWO

MAGNIFICENT DISTRACTIONS

The rickety rackety beep beep honk honk, the throngs of "here comes everybody" pulsing sheer aliveness in the heart of Saigon, recede.

Silence. A sound I've never heard. I'll just gaze into it.

The Trappist Abbey of Mont des Cats towers above Flanders fields. It is a steep climb to the abbey from the little village of Godewaersvelde, a trek made more of a challenge by the darkness and the falling snow. I start the climb at 3:00 a.m. hoping to be on time for Vigils at 4:00 a.m. I arrive just as the monks have assembled in the chill and darkness of the abbey church. I am breathless as the bell begins and we begin praying the psalms in the dark.

The monks know these prayers by heart. But among them, one or another casts a dim flashlight on a page of the

13

Psalter so as to lead the others through the words that cut deep even though they are spoken soft as whisper.

In the silence, I listen. Nothing more.

Behind and above the altar in this utterly simple Trappist abbey church there is a flickering light reminding all who gather that Christ's presence is never extinguished. I cannot take my eyes off the light. There is nothing else in this space, this place. There is only the light.

Memories are of memories, which are memories of memories. We can never retrieve or recollect an original experience, a "raw" experience. Our access to an original, "raw," experience is through memories remembered.

It was dark. In my parish church, Our Mother of Sorrows in the Irish Catholic ghetto of West Philadelphia, I was held in the arms of someone who loved me—too tiny to walk. And someone who loved the one who loved me was near me. There was whispering, a mix of Irish and English.

She pointed to the light. Looking toward the light, at the light, into the light, is my earliest memory. And their whisper, one in Irish, one in English: "God is there, up there; look at the light. God is near." Tá Dia anseo. "God is here."

It is a light that caressed my eyes and has lured, led me all this way, from Our Mother of Sorrows to the Trappist Abbey of Mont des Cats overlooking Flanders fields, where poppies do not blow in the cold and snow.

The light warms the silence of the space. Even and especially that space in me which, from infancy in arms until this moment, has longed to make enough room in the darkness: "God is there." "God is here." Far more than just a memory remembered as I sit in Silence gazing into the light.

The abbot and the novice master wondered aloud with me. They are concerned about the aging of the monks and the likelihood of fewer and fewer newcomers to the monastery. In predictable tones, their diagnosis pointed to a lack of willingness on the part of young people to make and keep commitments, the perils of the "dictatorship of relativism," and the evils of secularism. They ask only one question of me: What is the biggest obstacle today to living the contemplative life? In quasi-monastic fashion I answered with few words: "The Internet, and even more so, the smartphone."

They who had just struck out at the proverbial whipping boy of all the world's evils—secularism—rushed into defense position as they delineated the wonders of the Internet for attracting the young to the monastic life. Why, they wondered, is it an obstacle to a life of prayer? Weighing the wisdom of the *Sayings of the Desert Fathers*, which puts years, indeed decades, of self-knowledge into very few words, I put it this way: "With the Internet and the smartphone always at hand, you can be anywhere in the world you want to be, with whomever you want to be, at whatever time of day or night." I went on and took the risk of telling the abbot what he no doubt already knew: "The whole point of living prayerfully and, for the monk, the contemplative life, is to be where you are and nowhere else, day in and day out, and to stay alive to it. The key to living prayerfully is to be in your own skin, to be where you are and nowhere else, to learn how to look long and lovingly for the traces of God's nearness in human life, history, the world, and the Church." The challenge, I suggested in an attempt to end on a positive note, is to recognize that there are many benefits to the Internet and the smartphone. But, I added: The new recruits who may come to the monastery will do so after spending much of their life on the Internet, having given more attention to their smartphone than to their parents or teachers, and even their friends.

I tried to put it crisply: "It's all a *magnificent distraction*."

One who tries, not just to say one's prayers but to live prayerfully, knows that living with your "head down," fixated on a smartphone, and so many other magnificent distractions are obstacles, hurdles, to living prayerfully. They divert our attention from the first and final imperative of living prayerfully: Pay attention! As Simone Weil reminds: "Absolute attention is prayer." It is a never-ending discipline of learning how to look; learning how to listen long and lovingly to the beating of the heart of God. Be alert! Be attentive!

Turning away from these magnificent distractions makes room for entering the silence, that space, that place, that "nothing" which is found in freedom from distraction. Living prayerfully gives rise to the daily wondering if there is ever enough space/place, room enough for the Unfathomable Mystery whose horizon expands the closer we draw near to the encounter with the One whose name is above all naming.

The Spirit of God is present and active within the culture, the "lifeworld," of a people, no matter how depraved, debauched, decadent, or indifferent it may be thought to be. At work within a culture, the Spirit enlightens, enlivens, guides, and heals in such a way as to transform persons within a culture and, perhaps bit by bit, the culture itself, so that it more effectively furthers authentic human flourishing.

A human heart longing for an ever-deeper awareness of the divine presence does so in the face of cultural elements that can thwart, rather than cultivate, nurture, and sustain its desire. Such hurdles vary given a particular cultural matrix. Vietnam is not France is not Madagascar is not the Yukon is not Ecuador. No culture makes the heart's movement to God in prayer a free and easy ride. There are bumps, ditches, ravines that must be identified and navigated if we are to pray without ceasing, praying always. Again, this does not mean chattering to God from rising to sleeping. Rather, we ought not to be without prayer for even a single moment, praying day and night for the thousands. Here we can take heart in the words of the psalmist: "The Lord gives to the beloved even in sleep" (cf. Ps 127:2). Yes, even in sleep the heart at rest is a heart at prayer, quietly beating by the grace of God dwelling within.

There are particular hurdles that must be named and addressed as we respond to the invitation to live prayerfully. To recognize and delineate these is not to make the exhortation to "pray always" (1 Thess 5:17) seem an even more impossible task. It is, rather, to gain a clearer view of the terrain in which we find ourselves as the human heart longs for God in our own time and in our own place.

COLLISION SPEED

In *Let Us Dream: The Path to a Better Future* Pope Francis reminds us: "We need…a healthy capacity for silent reflection, places of refuge from the tyranny of the urgent." The first hurdle we must confront, if we can just slow down and pay attention, is the pace of life that most of us keep. Whatever our way or walk of life, we move through our days at breakneck speed. There are often long commutes to and from work. For most there are long hours at the workplace. There are children to be dropped off and picked up from daycare, or ballet practice, or softball, or soccer. After work and microwave dinner on-the-run or from a fast-food drive-through window, there are meetings of neighborhood committees, support groups, boards of all sorts. Many of us are on the brink of exhaustion much of the time. At the end of the day many are depleted of energy and can only plop in front of the TV. Even vacation time is one more thing we "do." If we really listen to one another, many, indeed most, are saying that they are too busy, and there are just not enough hours in a day. We are frenzied and frantic, breathlessly racing from one task to the next. So, who has time to pray?

We live in an unrelenting atmosphere of busyness. It is as if we are living in a pressure cooker most days—with the heat turned up full blast.

Racing through life at collision speed is one way of assuring that we likely won't arrive safely at our destination. Facing into this truth unflinchingly, how does one begin to be still long enough to attend to the presence of the God who is the Source and Ground of all that is, from whom springs the very life and lives we put at risk because of the speed with which we race through our days?

If this hurdle is to be overcome, attention is to be given to the basic human need for rest and leisure. At leisure, at rest, we think less, do less, and look more. Perhaps we even read—a BOOK!—that we hold gently in our hands, quietly turning its pages.

It is crucial to be attentive to a question that needs to be asked and answered each day: What am I doing when I am doing what I am doing? And why am I doing it? Answering this question may give us pause and help to prevent us from becoming doers unto death. Pondering this question and the answer that comes each day, we begin to quietly tuck away our craving for recognition of our achievements. We slowly cease trying to gain the love of others through the things we do for them. While at leisure, at rest, we can refrain from doing yet more. Painfully, we abandon ourselves to doing less and loving more from those depths deeper than any doing.

Living prayerfully is not just one more activity, one more thing to do. Prayer is a habit of being alert to the heart in ourselves and others, that capacity in all of us to be in relation with another, others, every living creature, and God. When this capacity is cultivated and disciplined, we become poised to recognize God's constant coming.

To follow the path of living prayerfully there is one crucial step we must take to move forward: STOP!

THE BOTTOM LINE

In our lifeworld, our culture, efficiency and productivity rank high on the list of priorities right alongside independence, self-sufficiency, and self-determination. Above all we want to stand on our own two feet. We want to know the hard facts and figures, "the bottom line." We are "doers." We strive and strain for achievement and success. Competition is woven into the cultural fabric. Many of us are driven, propelled by forces beyond our control, often having lost sight of why we are doing what we are doing. This presents real obstacles to prayer, which is never a matter of success and achievement. In authentic prayer, there may be a sense in which nothing is going on; a feeling that there is nothing to do. There is nothing to prove, nothing that can be won by our efforts. We cannot produce results. Even now, we want to know: What do I DO to live prayerfully?

Living prayerfully is something of an art. Ask an artist what she DOES to cast a "let it just kiss your eyes!" bronze. She will likely demur. It is not a matter of how much or how often one prays as it is a matter of how well one lives prayerfully. It requires the cultivation of a habit—slow, repetitive, steps to staying alive to it, being alert to life, to God's constant coming.

Efficiency in prayer involves abandonment, relaxing and letting God be God on God's own terms, as well as a willingness to accept life on life's terms rather than our own.

Moving more deeply into living prayerfully requires that we recognize:

I AM SO MUCH MORE THAN WHAT I DO.

CONGESTIVE CREATIVITY

Projects and plans give us something to work for, something to look forward to and, once achieved, a sense of satisfaction and fulfillment. But the appointment book in our briefcase, on the desk, on the kitchen wall, or on our smartphone can rule our lives. The smartphone has become a symbol of life in the early decades of the twenty-first century. We race from one thing to the next, finish one job, scratch it off the list, or delete it from our mobile phone, and then begin another task.

This often leaves little space in which the imagination and creativity can bloom. In prayerful living, imagination and creativity are given room. Setting priorities and accomplishing goals are not of the utmost importance when we live prayerfully.

Living prayerfully requires that our priority is paying attention, being alert. This is a tall order when we live in a "heads down" culture, a lifeworld in which most eyes are glued to smartphones.

When we give ourselves to prayerful living, there is nowhere to go, no task to be achieved, no mission to be accomplished. Part of the difficulty we face in living prayerfully is a sense of our own expendability, our uselessness. We often find ourselves asking: "What's the point? What am I doing here?" But prayer is not a project, something to be done, finished, like all the other projects in our lives. Nor does it unfold according to a plan or set of objectives. Its outcomes cannot be assessed. It is a sustained process of paying attention, being alert, staying alive to the source of all that is True, Good, and Beautiful, into whose heart we surrender day by day, until we breathe our last and—with the One who emptied himself in human flesh, unto death, and into hell—we commend ourselves without reserve and with boundless confidence into the Unfathomable Mystery he called Father.

The next step into living prayerfully:

Quit multitasking: *Age quod agis.* DO WHAT YOU ARE DOING. ONE BY ONE.

ISOLATION

One of the major problems that people in our culture face is a deep sense of disconnectedness, a lack of connection. Better: Being cut adrift. The effects of the breakdown of the nuclear family, increased mobility, massive urbanization, high-tech communication have all contributed to a seemingly chronic state of inability or unwillingness to take part in a shared way of life or community. There seems to be a large-scale failure to appropriate the values of a family, group, or community, resulting in an inability to identify with others and a strong inclination to want to stand apart.

Add to this the devastating effects of the COVID-19 pandemic, the effects of which will likely be "in our bones" for generations.

While prayerful living is something that springs from deep within one's heart, it is a dimension of human and Christian life which, for most of us, cannot thrive without the support of a community or a sense of belonging with others. To thrive we need to nestle into a spiritual home of some sort, even if it is with a small circle of others who share a common sense of meaning, value, and purpose.

Those who experience isolation, interruption, disconnection due to alcoholism, drug abuse, child abuse, sexual abuse, or violence often recognize the need for a circle of support offering self-help and mutual help. Alcoholics Anonymous, various Twelve-Step programs, and other support groups like them are based on the recognition that we cannot go it alone. For increasing numbers of people, the residue of the effects of the pandemic, the likes of which may catch us unawares again, remain. The wedge that has driven people and groups apart will not be quickly or easily healed.

Hard as it may seem, moving forward in living prayerfully requires that I dig deep and remember:

EVERYTHING IS RELATED TO EVERYTHING AND EVERYONE IS RELATED TO EVERYONE ELSE. EVEN ME.

QUICK AND EASY COMMUNIQUÉS

Prayer is often understood in terms of dialogue or interpersonal communication. Effective communication requires the ability to listen, to wait in an effort to allow the other to have room to speak, to listen to the other.

Ours is an age of instant communications. We watched the terrorist attack on the World Trade Center as it happened. We are able to sit in our living rooms as Russia invades Ukraine, the Hamas attack on Israel and Israel's retaliation NOW, or check our mobile phones to see which country or countries are being afflicted with systemic violence. We don't wait until we read about it in the evening newspaper (where can you find one of those these days?). The news—as it is happening now—is one finger-tip and one button away. There is no need to wait for the morning's local newspaper or a printed copy of the *New York Times*. Whatever the benefits of quick and easy com-munications may be, there is a downside: They are quite misleading and indeed detrimental if we expect prayer to yield quick and easy results.

We do not get quick information in prayer. There is no instant printout in answer to our constant questions. Our meager conundrums are not met with a ready reply, if indeed the reply we anticipate comes at all.

If prayer may be likened to dialogue, one needs to be willing to wait long and lovingly, to let oneself be put "on hold" and wait patiently and quietly for a response, often much longer than we would like. In waiting, the longing becomes the love.

Such an approach to prayer and prayerful living demands more than engaging the most rudimentary forms of praying. Prayerful living involves more than rattling off memorized prayers by rote, or speeding through decades of the rosary, or paging through one's holy cards and devo-tional prayerbook during Mass.

But what seems to be happening is that for many of our young, the memorization and rapid recitation of the simplest of prayers, such as the Hail Mary and the Our Father, have been set aside. And nothing has taken their place. This is to say nothing of the lack of rudimentary familiarity with the biblical story and with the Sacred Scrip-ture among the young. Immersed in the lifeworld of quick and easy communiqués, many are simply at a loss, not just for words, but for a single clue regarding how to cultivate an awareness of God's nearness by staying still, attentive to the silent Word beneath and beyond the unrelenting verbal tsunami that does not facilitate true communication, to say nothing of interpersonal communication. The current use of the term "reaching out" is not for the purpose of real communication, but for the transmission and reception of useful information. In just a few decades we have gone from fax (now out of date!) to email (who can be bothered checking their email any longer?) to text messages with links, downloads, videos, TV programs, and music—to say nothing of live pornography! It's all ours with a quick click and a fingertip. Why wait?

If we are to move forward in living prayerfully, perhaps the most important thing to learn is:

STOP. CALM DOWN. WAIT.

WITHOUT A COMPASS

Well beyond the lifeworld of the United States there is a widespread loss of confidence in leadership and authority. Paradoxically, there is a rise of authoritarian regimes in various parts of the world. Consider the debacle of the toppling of British Prime Minister Boris Johnson and the meteoric rise and demise of his successor, Prime Minister Liz Truss, both failing to GET BREXIT DONE in any satisfactory manner, as both had promised, leaving the hopes of the constituent countries of the United Kingdom dashed and its peoples far less united. The list goes on and on.

In our own country there is an astounding lack of civility and virtue across both political parties. The country is torn. What is needed is a true statesman or stateswoman in the strict and formal sense, someone who has proven character, vision, civic virtue, which are all sorely lacking on the current scene. Where to turn?

One might suggest that in the United States this erosion of confidence in leadership and authority began with the Watergate scandal. But its roots lie much deeper.

This is true not only regarding civil leaders but religious leaders as well. The credibility of leadership and authority in the Roman Catholic Church is diminished each time a priest is accused or convicted of pedophilia, and shattered altogether when it is disclosed that the bishop or religious superior had turned a deaf ear to the plea for help from a victim of abuse, or the family of a victim of sexual abuse. Where to turn? To whom shall we go?

In the face of the political disarray in which we are smothered, and alert to the silent but seismic schism underway in the Church, what is needed above all is a finely tuned interior compass.

But in recognizing and hurdling the obstacles to prayerful living unique to each culture, to each lifeworld, we would do well to seek and find those who have experience in the ways of prayer, who are recognized as trustworthy and wise guides, whose authority we can trust in leading us in the art of living prayerfully. Such wise guides are in short supply. While there has been a recognizable increase in the number of lay and ordained ministers trained in pastoral counseling, spiritual direction, and related fields, it is harder to determine just who and how many have real skill in praying themselves, so as to lead others on the way. To whom do we turn with confidence, especially when one's way and walk in life is to live prayerfully? Who, by virtue of being schooled in the life of prayer, can understand the heart of another, who knows with every inch and ounce of their being that one ought never, for moment, whether awake or asleep, be without prayer, praying day and night for the multitude, especially those who are poor and suffering in any way?

We are astonished when we see the suffering multitudes burst into prayer, such as the people of Haiti in the wake of yet another hurricane. Often there is more vibrant prayer among the suffering masses than in those places where people are at ease. Ever vigilant, the prayerful heart is alert to those whose numbers are beyond measure, whose unspeakable suffering makes it nearly impossible to pray, let alone to live prayerfully.

Moving forward in living prayerfully requires the recognition:

THE MOST RELIABLE COMPASS IS HIDDEN WITHIN.

CACOPHONY AND CLUTTER

Our lives are noisy and cluttered. It seems that every major city in the United States and around the world has become a land of eternal traffic. Big screen TVs in most rooms of the house, in the dentist's office, in the car repair shop. Blaring music that is not only harsh and dehumanizing with lyrics that, by any standards, are vulgar, is pumped/thumped into restaurants, supermarkets, bookstores and, yes, even libraries. Shopping malls and sports bars have replaced the town square or the city park—quiet, tranquil—as the places where people congregate. Requests to turn down the thumping music—sometimes with vulgar lyrics—are met with the disdainful rejoinder: "'Corporate' sets the rules for what we do here." Echoes of Big Brother!

We are drowning in a sea of endless noise. Our lives are cluttered with so much stuff, so many things. Our places, our spaces, are filled to the brim with "product," things, surplus. Even in a time of economic hardship, when we are struggling to make ends meet, the want to acquire more can get the upper hand with us.

There is no denying the importance of satisfying basic human needs. But in a materialist and consumerist culture such as ours, needs and wants are confused. Something in us craves more and more and more, propelled by some hunger that is insatiable: Will having one more of yet another thing finally satisfy us?

The spiritual stranglehold in which many of us are gripped is due in no small measure to the glut of noise and stuff that we have come to believe we simply cannot do without. Is "Alexa" really as necessary a member of the household as some would have us believe? More chatter! A color television in the living room, in the dining area, on the kitchen counter, in the bedroom(s), and in the bathroom?

The effect of materialism and consumerism is to render us very poor candidates for authentic prayer. For prayer is a movement of the heart, a desire which does not desire this or that object, thing, or sound. Authentic desire does not want more and more stuff. Praying entails the cultivation of a desire which desires only its own increase. True desire wants only to desire more desiring that in which, in whom, the heart will finally rest.

The meaning and purpose of prayerful living is found in the waiting for that which, the One who, is not a thing at all. In wanting to want God there is nothing to be gotten, nothing to be gained; indeed, no sound to be heard.

At this stage, moving forward in living prayerfully requires two things:

1. TUNE IT OUT, TURN IT DOWN, TURN IT OFF.
2. GET RID OF MOST OF YOUR STUFF BECAUSE NO ONE ELSE REALLY WANTS OR NEEDS IT!

CHAPTER THREE

SILENCE, SOBRIETY, SOLIDARITY

It is now long before dawn in the quiet of Flanders fields. Echoes of John McCrae: "In Flanders fields where poppies blow..." stir in me somewhere as I awaken early on a quiet Sunday morning. My little room is in a place called Godewaersvelde (some say it's Flemish for "God's fields"), right at the zigzag border between France and Belgium. The fields on both sides of the border are dotted with dozens of cemeteries housing the remains of casualties—French, Canadian, British, Belgian, American, Irish—of the Great War (the war to end all wars; ha!) and the Second World War.

The Vietnam War was the war of my generation. I am reminded that my parents were children of the Second World War. It marked them as the Vietnam War marked me. Today, this Sunday, is the fifth anniversary of the day my mother died, or better, made passage. She marked me and does so even now.

Wending my way on foot to the village church, I find the door open, even on a cold, damp, foggy morning in French Flanders. I go into the deep, dank darkness of this church so stark and spare. There is nothing distinctive about this place other than a banner over the altar. I squint to see the words: Ou est ton frère? *Where is your brother? I let those words drop down deep and nestle achingly alongside a wordless wonder stirring in me:* Et, toi, ou est ta soeur? *Where is your sister?*

I sit. Alone. Quiet. Alert. Waiting for God's constant coming.

Sometime later—who knows how long?—there are shuffles, whispers, the crinkles of heavy coats as the locals begin to assemble for Sunday Mass. Then a few instruments and a small choir practice the music of Taizé.

The locals continue to assemble. Perhaps there are twenty or thirty or forty. They sit on straight back wobbly little chairs in a circle close to the lectern and the altar.

These are les Ch'tis, *a simple, humble, farming people nestled in the heart of Flanders fields. They speak a dialect, some would say a language of their own, common in northern France. Alert to the difference in the language of* les Ch'tis *I am right smack-dab on the border of knowing and unknowing.*

Moments before the Mass begins, she arrives. She is dressed in a long white hooded christening gown, the likes of which I have not seen since my childhood. I wore one. So did all the children of my parish in the Irish Catholic ghetto of West Philadelphia in which I was reared in the fifties and early sixties.

The crisp white christening gown radiates warmth, as does she, Phillipa, who has been brought by her parents and godparents to this cold stone church. Unbeknownst to everyone gathered here, Philippa is to be baptized on the fifth anniversary of my mother's passage. She will be brought into the Body of Christ gathered here—member for member—in this place that is no place at all on anyone's map. Godewaersvelde. Even here the Word is speaking, and the Spirit is breathing in this "little place that God forgot."

There is Taizé music, a confident choir, and a congregation alert and active in all the movements of this eucharistic celebration in the wee hours of the morning.

At the appointed time, the priest comes forward into the congregation and stands before Philippa, her parents, her godparents. His words crack in my ears: Some Ch'ti; some French. He offers a brief admonition to Phillipa's parents, godparents, and all present. I stand silent. I am all eyes. Listening without fully comprehending, until his final few lines which circle back in French: "Philippa, now begins her journey of sanctity. But sanctity is not perfection. Sanctity is in desiring God."

Then her parents and godparents bring Philippa to the center of the church where there is a large bucket, perhaps four feet tall, filled with water. It's got to be cold!

Philippa is stripped naked and plunged into the water in the name of the Father, and of the Son, and of the Holy Spirt. How different from baptism in most countries in the West where a sprinkle, "a little dab will do ya," is the preference of most sacramental minimalists.

I weep. Quietly. Uncontrollably. I am being plunged into those bitter cold waters with Philippa. My mother is there/here. And my father. I went down into those waters as I do again on this bitter cold February morning in the land of these French-Flemish hillbillies, les Ch'tis.

Like Philippa today, I was unaware at the time of my baptism that I was embarking on the path to sanctity. My hope for Philippa is that she follows the path of sanctity wherever it may lead. May she learn day by day to follow the jalons de route, *the signposts along the way, to sanctity. And may she be quick to learn that those signposts along the way do not spell P-E-R-F-E-C-T-I-O-N. Rather, petite Philippa, the signposts to sanctity are now embedded in your soul. Within you. As you move through life, pay attention to the words we have heard today: "Sanctity is in desiring God." Wanting God. Longing for God. Or at least: Wanting to want God.*

"I baptize you in the name of the Father, and of the Son, and of the Holy Spirit." Some seventy years later those words drop down in me. Heard again in the silence of pre-dawn, in a church all stark and spare, in the presence of Philippa and her family...and my mother (RIP February 18, 2018).

We may be very good at "saying our prayers," true to our devotions, even fully, consciously, and actively participating in the celebration of the Eucharist. But that does not mean that we are praying unceasingly or living prayerfully.

Silence, Sobriety, Solidarity. Some approaches to prayer focus either on the "inner way" of quiet reflection,

recollection, meditation and so on, or on the "outer
of liturgy, evangelization, or social justice activity.
Silence and Sobriety may be thought of in terms of the
"inner way," Solidarity brings us necessarily through the
outer way of engagement with events, others, the world,
every living creature, indeed with all that lives. But entering into Silence, Sobriety, and Solidarity brings us to the
realization that this inner way versus outer way is a false
dichotomy.

Rather than moving through these three one by one
in sequence, there is an interplay of all three from the very
start. We do not begin in Silence, then experience Sobriety,
and only then know ourselves to be at one, in Solidarity,
with the other, others, every living creature, and God. In
the deepest kind of prayer, because we are sober (1 Pet 5:8)
we know ourselves to be one in the silence.

SILENCE

It's deafening.
I've heard
that wide open space of a whisper's echo.
Silence
a sound I've never heard.
I stand and stare at it.

The magnificent distractions exhaust us. We are distracted less by choice than by circumstance but distracted
nonetheless. We long for quiet, for deep rest, for distance

and space. It is only there and then that a still, small voice might be heard.

The payoff for rejecting, indeed driving out, these magnificent distractions is the space for silence and for a real, albeit often hidden, relationship with the One whose name above all naming is Love. Therein we reach for that place and that "nothing" that is found in freedom from distraction. The discipline, the "asceticism," of living prayerfully entails wondering day by day if we have left enough space within for the immensity of God and for that faint whisper.

In some languages, when you want to invite someone to your house you can say to them "come, stay." This might describe the key to "praying unceasingly." In the deepest kind of prayer, we are invited to *stay* still waiting in the presence of the Unfathomable Mystery. When there is nothing to say, you say nothing. And as we enter into the silence, there is nothing to say lest we break the silence. We stay, abide, remain in Silence.

The origins here are in the Greek verb *menò* (to stay, to abide, to remain, to dwell), a very important verb in the New Testament. In fact, the verb *menò* or its derivatives appears 118 times in the New Testament (from a total of 5,394 different words in the New Testament). When this verb is used in the Gospels, it bespeaks a certain degree of intimacy with Jesus.

For example, in the Gospel of John we find the two disciples of John the Baptist who went to ask Jesus where he was staying (see John 1:38). And Jesus says to them: "Come and see" (v. 39). And immediately after we are informed by the evangelist that they went and saw where Jesus *(menei)* and *they stayed* (*emeinan*) with him that da

In the Gospel of Luke, we find Jesus telling Zacchaeus: Zacchaeus, hurry and come down, for I must stay (*menai*) at your house today (see Luke 19:5).

Silence is not only the absence of sound or the quelling of cacophony both exterior and interior. Silence is also a place, the space of encounter. Here we encounter, we hear God's whisper in Silence. We enter Silence. When we enter this space, this place, named "Silence," we find that the encounter is already happening, because we are created by God, and it is God who first loves us and stirs up in us the longing for encounter with the One from whom we have come and to whom we shall return.

It is for each of us to work out, to make time and room enough for entering Silence.

In the place, the space, of Silence we hear God's whisper. But Silence is, just as much, a space or place of light. Here we see the traces of God's nearness. The eye squints. The traces are glimpsed one by one. As we draw nearer, the light brightens. The clearer and brighter the light, the more we see our own darkness. If Silence is the place, the space, of encounter with God, it is just as much the place of encounter with myself. And here, rather than turning away, we are summoned to stay, to remain, to abide. In darkness.

The heart of living prayerfully is staying still. And we only learn to do this in Silence. But prayerful living does not mean perpetual stillness, but a profound, thirsty restlessness that impels us to search again and again. Living prayerfully does not leave room for being preoccupied with ecstatic experiences but, rather, is attentive to the encounter with what life reveals and demands of us.

Silence is the space wherein the diversions we so often succumb to and the distractions that are an utter waste of our time and energy, are bid farewell. They depart, like demons driven out by the Son and Word of the Father who promised that the lame shall leap, the blind shall see, and the poor shall eat and have their fill.

Turning off, turning away from the magnificent distractions, the never-ending diversions on which we build so much, we realize that what we hear and what we see is so much nothing. It is the vastness and openness of the space where the eye does not rest but squints in search of something. But there seems to be only so much nothing. And, as if the lesson has never been learned by heart, the heart knows again as if for the first time: God is not a thing among other things. Not even the biggest and best of all possible things. God is NoThing. The NoThing encountered first and finally in Silence.

Facing out into so much nothing I snatch a glimpse of the beyondness of God. I am now and always rapt in attention to my unseen partner, the One whose name above all naming is Love.

Silence is not only a place or space of sweetness and light. It is also where we keep hidden those feelings, those events, those memories we would rather not face and rather not allow others to know. Silence can sometimes be a screen by which our deepest secrets are kept hidden from the eyes of others as well as from our own.

There is no way to the light but through the darkness of our own heart. There we must stay, abide, remain, wait for a deeper knowledge of our own darkness. The encounter we anticipate in Silence entails waiting and moving through our own darkness.

This darkness is all too easily thought of in the overly simplistic language of sin—what I have done and what I have failed to do. And that it surely is. But even more, staying in the darkness allows me to see the ways in which life has formed me and, more so, deformed me.

Life both forms and deforms me. No one escapes life's deformation. And all too often our identity formed around deformation. It is only by waiting long and lovingly in the silence, in the darkness, that I can see my life, the truth of my life, my life as a whole, in God.

Waiting long and lovingly, the light comes, just as sure as the rising of the sun. In that light I see my own life among mortals awash in God's love and mercy. Standing apart from our magnificent distractions, it is possible to see one's past in light of God's unrestricted forgiveness and to glimpse a future in which one can pass through the gates of suffering, dying, and death in peace. Here between the darkness and the light, this border between mortality and immortality, we let go of projects, of the inordinate need to control events and change others. We cease trying to chart the course of what may happen in the future, to our reputation, going so far as trying to manipulate the memories people might have of us. All of it is just so much nothing!

Staying still in the silence I encounter the One whose name above all naming is Love. I am able to face into death with no firm grasp of what lies ahead, what afterlife might be like, except that we shall be wholly immersed in the life-world of the loving God who sent the Beloved Son and gave us the Spirit who dwells in our hearts, in our communities, in all creation, in every living thing, throughout the universe. And that is enough.

SOBRIETY

Scholars and students of Christian spirituality often note that the 12-step program, originally of Alcoholics Anonymous, is the most significant contribution of the twentieth-century United States to the broad field of spirituality. The 12-step program, the contours of which are widely known, is at the heart of this spirituality. Even though the 12 steps have been applied to address various sorts of problematic behaviors such as compulsive overeating and addictions to life-threatening drugs such as opium or heroin, the goal of every 12-step program is sobriety.

"Getting sober," "staying sober," and the very notion of sobriety itself are tethered to alcohol and its abuse. But the notion of sobriety need not be understood as related to this single reference. In the biblical sense of the term, *sobriety* means living with a single-minded focus. Sobriety is akin to Kierkegaard's understanding of purity of heart as willing one thing.

In a night prayer said by many Christians throughout the world, there is a brief reading from 1 Peter 5:8: "Be sober and vigilant. Your opponent the devil is prowling around like a roaring lion looking for [someone] to devour."

Sobriety in the spiritual life has been referred to in different ways throughout the Christian tradition. Sobriety is poverty of spirit, purification, simplicity, modesty of mind, custody of the eyes, living with less so that others may live. But in using the term "sobriety," the focus is not only the self. The emphasis is twofold: (1) stripping away (or being stripped of) all that gets in the way of clarity; (2) avoiding indulgence through the rightly ordered disposition toward and the measured use of the goods of the earth.

How do I get sober? Just as there are twelve steps to AA and related programs, there are practices in the spiritual life. Not only are these five disciplines pertinent to spiritual sobriety. They are also helpful ingredients in the exercise of prudence in our day-to-day dealings in our everyday lives.

First, by paying attention we *recognize* what is before us, whether it is an object, a thought, an event, a conversation. We must decide whether it is good or yet another distraction from what matters.

Second, because the answer to the above may not be immediately apparent, the best course is almost always to exercise *restraint*.

Third, we *refrain* from moving forward unless and until there is sufficient clarity. More often than not, waiting is the better part of wisdom.

Fourth, we *refuse*: what is not good; what is yet another distraction; what is excessive in the way of food and drink; what is unnecessary in the way of creature comforts and endless accoutrements; what is a waste of time; what is idle chatter and gossip; what contributes to a never-ending cycle of negative thinking.

Fifth, we begin to experience a sort of *regeneration*. There is more energy, more joy, more light, more life.

Sometimes ever so slowly, the clouds break, the fog lifts. The cobwebs of my mind and heart seem to loosen. I can move freely again. I wake up. Alert. Sober. I am aware that I am perceiving differently. I see beyond my old, distorted, foggy way of seeing the other, others, and God. And I begin to see through and beyond myself both formed and deformed by my experience of life. I perceive differently. I can see! I see the truth, the truth of my life as a whole, in God.

We begin to discover what matters. Slowly we begin to peel away what is not essential or, at least, to see the distractions for what they are: the emails, voicemails, meetings, reports, assessments, mini- and pseudo-crises, tensions, headaches, "time sensitive" and urgent agenda items, overnight deliveries, the tsunami of text messages, Zoom conferences, video calls, FaceTime, and all those pressing "issues"—that worn-out, used-up, tired idiom of our hyper- and overpsychologized epoch. Each of us must face into the question of how and to what measure all of these may be nothing more than distractions from living with single-minded focus, being vigilant, sober, and alert to what really matters.

Stripping away, or being stripped of, all that gets in the way of the essential, there is more space and time for listening, for reflection, for reading, for moving more deeply into the Unfathomable Mystery always beyond my reach, the One for whom my heart longs. When I am sober, I see clearly that each and every distraction is so much nothing in light of the single most important truth at the heart of Christian life: I am a child of God. God's own son. You are God's own daughter; God's own son.

But the roaring lion is never very far. Indeed, at times, only a heartbeat away. Stay sober and alert!

SOLIDARITY

One of the most important things to learn in life is knowing how to not know. This is not the same as simply not knowing but actually learning how to not know: admitting, accepting, and embracing our limits. One of the first things to be learned in our approach to God is that in our relationship to God we must embrace the tensive interaction between knowing and not knowing. God is not to be known through the powers of the mind.

But the Unfathomable Mystery whose very being is Love in superabundant gift can be glimpsed, tasted, pursued in the desire of the human heart which longs in love for Love itself. Our encounter with the mystery of God can only commence in earnest once we accept that our stumbling does not cease but is ongoing.

Staying still in Silence, stripped of all the magnificent distractions, we await God's constant coming, an encounter not all at once but already always taking place within us, because the One from whom we come and to whom we shall return is dwelling within us. But who is this One already within us yet always exceeding our grasp?

This One calls us closer, to enter more deeply into the regions of incomprehension and unknowability. Beyond our seeing and our hearing springs the Word from beneath the words: the Mystic Name. The name beyond all naming: "I am who am." This is the unspeakable name breathed into those who have learned how to wait, how to hope, in the silence that makes no room for magnificent distractions.

This One is Unfathomable Mystery. "Mystery" often conveys a sense of unintelligibility bordering on nonsense. But real mystery is that which invites and allures us into fuller participation, all the while exceeding our want to grasp it, hold on to it, contain it. Mystery is always more, always ahead of us, inviting us to greater life, light, and love. But we gain glimpses; we hear whispers. Most unfathomable of all is that the Mystic Name, "I am who am," is not an "I" at all. We are spiritually gobsmacked.

God is not an "I." God is not an individual. God is not *a* person. God does not exist as an isolated one or a being-turned-in-on-itself. "Father" is not God's proper name. Nor is "God" God's name. God has no proper name. "Father," "Son/Word," "Spirit/Love" are names that designate relationships: A father is only a father in relation to a son or daughter. A son or daughter is called that by virtue of his or her relation to a father or mother. And love is not self-contained but always toward and for another or others.

God is inexhaustible mystery. Unfathomable. Yet God is personal, that is, related—Father, Son/Word, Spirit/Love—always toward the other, toward us, for us, with us, and in us. God is personal, that is, God is sheer loving relation in self-gift; that self-giving, mutuality, and interdependence of the Three in One Love, are at the very heart of God's being, the "I am who am." God exists in a communion of persons toward one another in self-giving love, revealed in Son/Word and Spirit/Love in Silence and Sobriety. But it does not end there.

The relationality of the Three bonded in the One Love spills out over into a relationality with the world, thereby making it possible for human persons in relation to all creation to enter into this communion in the One Love.

The longest journey inward leads outward. In the presence of the Mystic Name we come to a deeper recognition that we come from others, and even in the deepmost depths of solitude, we live with others.

The "I" is not a self-contained being who at some stage in life chooses or elects to be in relationship with another and others. Solidarity is etched into our very being. From the very first moment of existence the infant is toward the other, ordinarily the mother or father, who is in turn toward and for the infant. From our origin we are related: we are from others, by others, toward others, for others, just as it is in God to exist in the relations of interpersonal love. The self-determination, independence, and autonomy we seek to maintain at all costs are seen anew in light of the recognition that we are not autonomous. We are from God, toward God, for God, that is, *theonomous.*

And what is true of human life is also true of everything that lives, of every inch and ounce of creation. The tiny agate as well as the ever-so-distant spray of stars are all related one to another, shimmering in the light of the One who is not one but Three in One Love.

God is not a Lone Being but Love itself. And in Love's embrace, as the love of the mother embraces her child from the very first moment, I know that I am not alone.

What is this strange and elusive thing that we name love? Quite simply, it is life pouring itself forth. To say that God is love is to say that God is not enclosed, turned in on self. God is the life that pours itself forth: constantly, abundantly, excessively, never-to-stop-coming-as-gift. Life is altogether and absolutely gift: a gift come freely. Unexpectedly. Undeservedly. This gift is constant. Trustworthy.

In Silence and Sobriety, I am held by the One whose Mystic Name, "I am who am," is not one but Three in One Love. In the embrace of Love itself I know myself to be at one, in solidarity with all humanity, with every living creature, with all creation. Love is trustworthy, and we are entrusted with the care of, dare I say responsibility for, all that has been given to us as gift.

In the face of God's never-ending coming, God's constant coming, as gift, I stand back, I fall back, into the silence. I am once again in that space of both darkness and light. In that place, rid of all the magnificent distractions, I see all that has gone before, in my own life, in history, in the world, and in the Church. The One whose name is above all naming is Love who has been there all along. And even before. In Silence, still I am heartsick in the face of the tsunami of human suffering, disease, famine, violence, war, and so much more—then and now. And ever shall be until God is all in all. My gaze turns from the darkness, through the darkness, to the light both within and without myself. Everything that lives and breathes is from God, toward God, for God, even and especially the last, the lost, the littlest, and the least of everyone and everything created in the image of the God who is not a Lone Being but the Three in One Love. Everything and everyone are related to everything and everyone else.

There are glimmers of hope for what is yet to come as I abide in Silence, Sobriety, and Solidarity. It is there,

here, in that region of wound and wisdom—the heart—whose geography is known only to the One who is called upon by the Mystic Name of Love, "I am who am," and "I shall be who I shall be," in hope I can believe against hope, and listen to the whisper echoing in my heart: *Dum spiro, spero*....While I breathe, I hope.

EPILOGUE

Borders. They mark. They distinguish. They separate. I sit at the border. Fluid, almost invisible, like the border in Franco-Flanders. But this border does not cross through God's fields, Godewaersvelde. It crosses through the badlands of West and Southwest Philadelphia, the neighborhoods of my childhood. I have come, once again, for the funeral of another cousin, several years my junior. His parents have already buried one child and a grandchild. All three gone due to the ravages of what I call loose and liquid living.

It is the time of year for ringing out Alleluias, poised as we are between Easter and Pentecost. Even in this simple funeral service in the small parlor of a nondescript funeral home there is reference to the One who is risen, source of our hope. And our joy.

Gazing at the urn containing my cousin's ashes, I cannot help but remember another border. The hard and seemingly never-ending border between Northern Ireland and the Republic of Ireland that claimed the lives of two other cousins during "The Troubles," wounding the soul of the Island of Ireland with scars ever so visible, even to this day.

Each of these cousins lived a life that no one would want to emulate. Two to alcohol, drugs, and addictions of all sorts. Another to drug addiction and gun violence. The lives of two others cut short in the conflict and violence caused by the cruelly imposed border that separates two opposing countries on one tiny island.

The life of each one was tragic by any standards, bringing incalculable pain and suffering to those near them as they dwelt among the living in the circles of hell. Yet, those they left behind would rather have them back at any cost. But each one crossed a border into the badlands from which there was no return.

Surrounded by mourning parents, brothers, sisters, nieces, nephews, and more, I gaze upon the ash-filled urn. They do not weep for naught. On the face of it, the life of the one we gather to mourn was misguided and warped. A disaster. But there was goodness, kindness, generosity, and good humor. Beneath it all there was mystery and beauty —a terrifying and terrible beauty.

As the mourners leave, I remain. At the border in the badlands. In the silence. More borders. I see the millions breathlessly struggling in the grip of poverty, violence, and persecution, crossing borders often at great risk, seeking survival—some would say better lives—for themselves and their families. In desperation they risk their lives and those of their loved ones for what they hope lies beyond their own badlands, racing to break out of the steel-clad cycles of suffering, injustice, and tragedy.

Millions are trapped in the circles of hell here and now, gasping for breath, begging for life. In these circles of hell, hunger is still a daily reality for millions, grinding poverty forces them to live in squalor. No education. No opportunity. No way out.

These circles of hell are erected in granite by the self-interest of others who ignore the common good, or use dishonest practices, political power, or violence to advance personal interests. Trapped within the granite walls of these circles of hell, millions die of neglect and disease while those outside the walls prosper and flourish. All the while, wars and terrorism claim the lives of countless innocent men, women, and children. Social inequities are woven into the fabric of societies. Numbers beyond the counting are ruled by others with little concern for human rights or providing opportunity for their people. The vulnerable, the disabled, the "unproductive" elderly are considered expendable, disposable...tossed into the dustbin of history's unknown. Or better, forgotten. Yes, it's better to forget them.

And then there are the circles of hell of our own making, the borders of our own building: resentment, impatience, intolerance, envy, greed, lust. The ingredients vary. The results are usually the same: we fail to live in right relationship with ourselves, the other, others, other living beings, and God. We are cut off. Walled in by self-absorption, self-preoccupation, and self-fixation, impermeable borders that others dare not cross.

In the silence of a vacant funeral parlor...the flowers have been taken, their sweet scent is gone, the urn has been removed, the mourners on their way to gather for a repast...I remember another. The One who crossed the border into the unfathomable darkness to gather those judged to be beyond hope.

Central to Christian belief, but often ignored or neglected, is the affirmation that at his death, Jesus descended among the dead. Some depictions of Christ's Pasch show him being raised from the tomb to the right hand of the Father in such a way that it blurs a creedal affirmation central to Christian faith and life since the earliest days of the Church. At his death, Christ does truly die, descending among the dead, into the "limbo of the fathers" (limbus patrum). In the earliest faith of the Church, Christ is thoroughly active in the underworld, engaged with liberating those long forgotten—surely Adam and Eve and their line. But the multitudes of their progeny sitting in darkness are not forgotten by God and are touched by the life, light, and love crossing the border into the netherworld.

Day by day, or week by week, we proclaim: Christ has died, Christ is risen, Christ will come again.

But the heart wonders: Does Christ still descend among the dead? Does Christ dwell here in the silence and lifelessness of an empty funeral home? In the empty hearts of those who mourn the loss of a life lost to loose and liquid living? In the circles of hell that lock in millions? At the borders of the badlands throughout the world? In my own heart that is strangled in darkness day by day even as it longs for the light?

In speaking of the Eucharist, the American novelist Flannery O'Connor once remarked: "If it's just a symbol, to hell with it." In the sacraments—in bread, wine, water, and oil—the incarnation of God's Love continues. We—member *for member—are his Body. Daily we rise and daily we die. And daily we descend with him. Before we ascend with him.*

Here at the invisible border of the badlands, at the edge of comprehension, there are still echoes of Easter's Alleluia. They are hard to hear. Living in Silence, Sobriety, and Solidarity brings us closer to the truth of what and where we are living. We are not yet fully a resurrection people until all of us, member for member, are brought together in the Christ who will be all in all. And until such time, our Alleluia is not to be full-throated.

While we live we must face into the truth that we are always somewhere between Good Friday and Easter Sunday. Between cross and resurrection. We are Sabbatarians, a people of the Saturday. Holy Saturday. Here we encounter the One for whom we long in Silence, Sobriety, Solidarity. In poised spiritual liberty we are given the grace to live long and lovingly between the Friday and the Sunday. This is the moment, here is the place, where God's reach goes deep, extending Love's hand beyond any and all borders, never losing sight of those who seem absolutely and utterly beyond hope. In hope we believe against hope (cf. Rom 4:18).

SUGGESTED READINGS

Ruth Burrows. *Essence of Prayer*. Mahwah, NJ: Hidden Spring, 2006.

Pope Francis. *Let Us Dream*. New York: Simon and Schuster, 2020.

Pope Francis. *Fratelli Tutti* (2020). https://www.vatican.va/content/francesco/en/encyclicals/documents/papa-francesco_20201003_enciclica-fratelli-tutti.html.

Pope Francis. *Gaudete et Exsultate* (2018). https://www.vatican.va/content/francesco/en/apost_exhortations/documents/papa-francesco_esortazione-ap_20180319_gaudete-et-exsultate.html.

Thomas Keating. *Open Mind, Open Heart*. London: Bloomsbury Continuum, 2019.

André Louf. *The Cistercian Way*. Kalamazoo, MI: Cistercian Publications, 1983.

———. *In the School of Contemplation*. Collegeville, MN: Cistercian Publications, 2015.

————. *Mercy in Weakness: Meditations on the Word.* Kalamazoo, MI: Cistercian Publications, 1998.

————. *Teach Us to Pray: Learning a Little about God.* Cambridge, MA: Cowley Publications, 1992.

Thomas Merton. *New Seeds of Contemplation.* New York: New Directions, 1961.

Karl Rahner. *Encounters with Silence.* South Bend, IN: St. Augustine's Press, 1999.

————. *The Need and Blessing of Prayer.* Collegeville, MN: Liturgical Press, 1997.

James Walsh, ed. *The Cloud of Unknowing.* New York: Paulist Press, 1981.

Benedicta Ward, SLG, ed. *The Sayings of the Desert Fathers: The Apophthegmata Patrum; The Alphabetic Collection.* Collegeville, MN: Liturgical Press, 1975.